Original title:
Quieted Breezes Along the Phoenix Rack

Copyright © 2025 Swan Charm
All rights reserved.

Author: Sara Säde
ISBN HARDBACK: 978-1-80559-376-8
ISBN PAPERBACK: 978-1-80559-875-6

Soft Whispers of Eternal Rebirth

In the dawn where shadows fade,
Blossoms breathe in gentle hues.
Every heart begins to wake,
Nature sings a tune so true.

Beneath the sky's embracing light,
Petals shimmer with each dew.
Echoes of a dream take flight,
As the world begins anew.

Life unfurls with every breeze,
Softly dancing through the grass.
Moments held in timeless ease,
Whispers of the future pass.

Branches sway in sweet refrain,
Birds alight in joyous song.
Underneath the falling rain,
Hope's resilience will grow strong.

Through the cycles, love will thrive,
In the silence, blessings swell.
From the dark, we all arrive,
Rebirth casts its sacred spell.

Voice of Ashes in the Evening's Glow

In the twilight's warm embrace,
Ashes dance in flickering light.
Whispers soft with mournful grace,
Stories linger through the night.

Flickers catch the fading breath,
Softest sighs from fire's past.
Echoes of a dance with death,
Memories in shadows cast.

Stars awaken in the sky,
Tales of love and loss unfold.
In the ash, they softly lie,
Timeless truths in whispers told.

With each ember's glowing thread,
Fragments of a life once lived.
In this silence, hearts are fed,
Balance found in what we give.

Beckoning through ashen dreams,
Cinders flicker, rise, and fall.
In the glow, the spirit seems,
To transcend the dark for all.

Luminous Silence Over the Cinder Sea

In the hush where shadows blend,
Cinder waves caress the shore.
Silent whispers, love will send,
Carried deep forevermore.

Glistening under moonlit gaze,
Stars reflect on liquid glow.
Time dissolves in tranquil haze,
Where the heart's true rivers flow.

Dreams unfold like sails at dawn,
Guiding whispers through the night.
Every mist a gentle yawn,
Cradling souls in softest light.

Through the silence, echoes ring,
Voices lost in velvet deep.
While the cinder sea will sing,
Songs of love the heart will keep.

Luminous paths through distant skies,
Connect the realms of now and then.
In this stillness, time defies,
Awakening our hearts again.

Ethereal Winds of a Celestial Dust

In the hush of starry nights,
Ethereal winds gently play.
Carrying dreams on their flights,
Guiding souls along the way.

Whispers travel through the dark,
Soft as petals, light as air.
Every moment leaves a mark,
Secrets told with tender care.

Celestial dust in silver beams,
Sparks of life and warmth collide.
In the depths of woven dreams,
We find solace, hearts abide.

Through the cosmos, spirits roam,
Seeking love in endless space.
In the winds, we find our home,
Wrapped in beauty, endless grace.

Let us dance in starlit skies,
Bathe in whispers of the night.
In the heart, the universe lies,
Eternal bonds of love and light.

Hidden Murmurs by the Edge of Time

In shadows deep where whispers play,
The echoes stir, a fleeting day.
Time drifts slow, a silent rhyme,
In hidden murmurs, lost in time.

Beneath the stars, the secrets dwell,
Each heartbeat tells a silent bell.
The moonlight drapes a silver line,
A constant dance, the edge of time.

In twilight's breath, the moments sigh,
The past and future weave and tie.
With tender grace, they intertwine,
In soft reflections, fate's design.

When silence speaks, the world holds still,
Intangible, an unseen thrill.
In shadowed whispers, dreams align,
The essence waits, the edge of time.

And as we walk through realms so vast,
The fleeting moments whisper past.
A gentle touch, a subtle sign,
In hidden murmurs, all is fine.

The Emblem of Solitude in Flaming Whispers

In quiet realms where shadows blend,
A solitude that knows no end.
The flames they dance, a vivid sign,
In flaming whispers, hearts entwine.

Alone beneath the starry dome,
The ember's glow, a hearth, a home.
Within the silence, sparks align,
The emblem waits, in flames, it shines.

Lost in the echoes of the night,
The flickering flames, a ghostly light.
In solitude, the soul will find,
A fiery thread that binds the mind.

Each whispered secret, softly cast,
A tapestry of futures past.
In fiery dreams, the heart confined,
An emblem glows, in flames, designed.

So let the night embrace the flame,
In solitude, no need for fame.
The whispers carry tales benign,
In flaming whispers, love's divine.

Flickering Flames in Silent Air

In the dark where shadows dance,
Flickering flames, they take a chance.
Whispers soft, a secret's glow,
In silent air, the embers flow.

Night's embrace, a tender spark,
Lighting dreams from out the dark.
With each flicker, stories told,
Of warmth and heart, of brave and bold.

Crisp and clear, the evening sings,
Carried forth on smoky wings.
In the stillness, a perfect chance,
To find the joy in fate's fine dance.

Around the fire, we gather near,
Comfort shared, and hearts sincere.
In flickering light, we feel alive,
In silent air, our spirits thrive.

The Gentle Veil of Autumn's Breath

Whispers of leaves in golden hues,
Autumn's breath, a world ensues.
Gentle winds through branches weave,
Nature's canvas, hard to leave.

Crisp allure of morning's light,
Sweeping dreams from day to night.
Softly falling, time drifts by,
As seasons turn and echoes sigh.

Beneath the boughs, a quiet peace,
In every rustle, sweet release.
Colors merge, a warm embrace,
In autumn's arms, we find our place.

Every path adorned in lace,
Of fiery shades, a slow-paced race.
With every step, the whispers call,
In nature's heart, we feel it all.

Calm Shadows on the Desert's Edge

Underneath the vast, clear sky,
Calm shadows rest as day slips by.
Sands of gold and whispers low,
Bounce off mountains, silent glow.

Windswept tales of lost romance,
In quiet nights, the stars entrance.
Footprints fade, but dreams remain,
In desert's hush, we bear the strain.

Each grain speaks of ancient lore,
In stillness found, we crave for more.
Beneath the moon's soft, silver light,
We find our way, our spirits bright.

Time stands still on this vast land,
Where calm shadows stretch and stand.
In every whisper, life's embrace,
On desert's edge, we find our place.

Soft Serenades of the Feathered Night

When twilight falls and silence grows,
Soft serenades, the night bestows.
Chirps and trills, a gentle sound,
In shadows deep, where dreams abound.

Beneath the stars, the world transforms,
Birds take flight, as magic swarms.
With every note, the heart takes flight,
In feathered whispers, pure delight.

The moon above a watchful eye,
Guiding songs that weave and fly.
In harmony, the night sings sweet,
Where every heart and rhythm meet.

Lost in sound, we drift away,
To twilight's tune, where wishes play.
In soft serenades, dreams ignite,
In feathered night, all feels so right.

Whispers of the Wandering Wind

Through the trees it softly glides,
Carrying tales from distant tides.
A gentle touch on cheek and brow,
It speaks of places far somehow.

Beneath the stars, it weaves a song,
In quiet nights where dreams belong.
Unraveled secrets on its breath,
Echoes of life, or whispered death.

With every gust, a memory flies,
Painting stories across the skies.
It stirs the leaves in joyous play,
Yet carries sorrow far away.

It dances softly on the hills,
Awakens silence, sparks new thrills.
In every nook, it finds its home,
The wandering wind, forever roams.

Stillness Beneath the Ember Sky

Underneath the glowing embers,
Stillness wraps the night like members.
Each flicker is a whispered prayer,
Carried softly through the air.

Shadows linger by the fire's light,
Embraced by warmth, dispelling fright.
Time stands still as moments freeze,
In harmony with rustling leaves.

The stars awaken, blink and sigh,
Painting dreams where wishes lie.
The earth breathes deep in tranquil peace,
A gentle balm that brings release.

Wrapped in night's eternal cloak,
Thoughts unfurl like wisps of smoke.
In this stillness, hearts align,
Finding solace in the divine.

Murmurs of the Waking Dawn

First light breaks the dark embrace,
Awakens day with gentle grace.
Murmurs rise from slumber's keep,
As nature stirs from tranquil sleep.

A chorus born of rustling leaves,
Whispers of hope that night deceives.
Birds tune their voices, sweet and clear,
Proclaiming dawn is finally here.

Soft rays dance on dewy blooms,
Painting gold on hallowed rooms.
Each moment, fresh, a new design,
Invites us to the warm sunshine.

Clouds drift lazily, basking slow,
While shadows lengthen, ebb and flow.
In the hush, the world reveals,
The magic that the dawn conceals.

Hushed Echoes of Distant Flames

Flickering softly in the night,
Echoes of warmth, a soft delight.
Distant flames whispering tales true,
Of hearts entwined and love anew.

Beneath the stars, they flicker bright,
Casting shadows, weaving light.
Memories held in glowing red,
In silent moments, softly said.

Stories linger in the air,
Of laughter shared and tender care.
With every crackle, dreams ignite,
A tapestry of day and night.

Time bends close, as embers fade,
Layering warmth in twilight's shade.
In the hush, the whispers flow,
Of love and loss, the fire's glow.

Twilight's Embrace on an Ocean of Ash

On the horizon, colors blend,
Shadows stretch, as daylight ends.
Waves whisper tales of lost time,
In twilight's embrace, all feels sublime.

Stars awaken, one by one,
Under the glow of the fading sun.
Softly the night begins to weave,
A tapestry of dreams to conceive.

Ghostly figures dance on the shore,
As memories linger, forevermore.
Each glimmering spark in the deep,
Holds secrets of sorrow and peace to keep.

The salt-kissed breeze carries sighs,
A lullaby from the ashen skies.
Echoes of laughter and tears confined,
In an ocean of ash, they intertwine.

Beneath the veil of the coming dark,
Life's embers flicker, and hope leaves a mark.
In the twilight's embrace, find your way,
As night unfolds, guiding to the day.

Ashen Skies Sing with Subtle Breezes

Above, the heavens wear a shroud,
With whispers soft, they speak aloud.
Clouds in silence drift and soar,
Painting the world, forevermore.

Gentle breezes caress the ground,
Stirring the ash with a haunting sound.
Touched by shadows, the earth weeps,
In the memory of what it keeps.

Crimson glimmers fight the dusk,
In the decay, there's trust and rust.
Soft sighs travel through the trees,
Melting away with the evening's tease.

Each fading note a tale untold,
Of moments cherished, brave and bold.
Amidst the echoes, find your tune,
As ash falls gently beneath the moon.

In the stillness, hear the call,
Of ashen skies that cradle all.
Breathe in the night, let worries cease,
For subtle breezes whisper peace.

The Calm Before the Night's Renewal

The sun bows low, the world holds breath,
In twilight's grip, we dance with death.
A hush envelops, shadows grow,
As the calm prepares for the night's show.

Colors fade, the light is shy,
A brilliant canvas now says goodbye.
Hope lingers in the thickening air,
Anticipation laced with gentle care.

Stars ignite, an urgent plea,
To guide the lost, to set them free.
In the stillness, hearts align,
Ready for magic, the world's design.

The wind whispers secrets of old,
Stories of courage, timeless and bold.
A moment suspended, fragile yet bright,
The calm before the night's renewal light.

Unseen forces start to rise,
With every shadow, the spirit flies.
Embrace the night's enchanting song,
For in its depths, we all belong.

Reflections on the Wings of Inception

In the silence, dreams take flight,
Thoughts unfurl in the gentle night.
Mirrored moments kiss the dawn,
On wings of inception, we are drawn.

Ripples dance on the surface clear,
Each reflection whispers what we fear.
The past and future intertwine,
In every heartbeat, truth aligns.

Awakening thoughts, like fragile glass,
Break boundaries formed as shadows pass.
Traveling through the vast unknown,
Finding solace where we're alone.

In every glance, a story hides,
In echoes of laughter where hope resides.
With every breath, we begin anew,
On the wings of morning, dreams pursue.

Through the currents of time we glide,
In reflections deep, we must confide.
Unseen paths lay in front of me,
On wings of inception, we can be free.

The Color of Stillness in a Fiery Dream

In shadows deep, where silence reigns,
Crimson and gold, like whispered chains.
A touch of peace in chaos bright,
Stillness dances in the night.

Amidst the blaze, a quiet hue,
A tranquil heart, steadfast and true.
Soft as feathers in a warm embrace,
Time slows down in this sacred space.

Where flames may flicker, shadows loom,
The color still sings, dispelling gloom.
Dreams awaken, alive and bold,
Stories of warmth begin to unfold.

In fiery realms, a calm persists,
A gentle touch, a fleeting kiss.
Moments drift like whispers in air,
Painting serenity everywhere.

From blazing skies to softest dew,
The color of peace breaks through anew.
In the heart of the storm, a quiet gleam,
Lingers long in a fiery dream.

Echoes in the Hollow of Lost Horizons

Whispers of time in fading light,
Lost horizons, shadows of night.
Echoes dance on the edge of dreams,
Silent tales in moonlit beams.

In valleys deep, where memories wane,
Every heartbeat recalls the pain.
A hollow sound from ages past,
Promises made, yet none could last.

Winds of change through the stillness sigh,
Carrying dreams that drift and fly.
Across the void, a fleeting grace,
Hope finds solace in empty space.

The stars align in distant skies,
Glimmers of truth in endless lies.
They guide the lost, they light the way,
Through echoes faint, we find our stay.

With every step, the past is near,
Whispering softly, yet crystal clear.
In the hollow, where time unfolds,
Barriers break and stories told.

Quiet Whispers in the Heart of Fire

In the heart of flames where shadows play,
Quiet whispers beckon and sway.
Heat like a breath, warmth in flow,
Secrets shimmer, quietly glow.

Embers crackle, but softly hum,
In the quiet, a sacred drum.
Crimson dances, a passionate lure,
The heart of fire feels so pure.

Amidst the blaze, a soft refrain,
Words unspoken, yet full of gain.
A flicker bright, a longing sigh,
In the depths, the soul will fly.

Through the heat, a gentle stream,
Whispers cradle each fervent dream.
In the dance of flames, we find our bliss,
Embracing the warmth in every kiss.

As the fire crackles, we become one,
Magic ignites in the setting sun.
Quiet whispers, a soul's desire,
Forever bound in the heart of fire.

Time's Breath Between the Flames and Ash

Between flames and ash, time takes a breath,
A fragile dance that flirts with death.
Seconds linger, like glowing sparks,
Whispers of life in fading arcs.

In the heart of chaos, calm resides,
Through the ashes, a spirit guides.
Moments pause, where dreams collide,
In the stillness, hope will abide.

With every flicker, a story wanes,
Memories held in ethereal chains.
The ember's warmth, the chill of night,
Time's breath rests, just out of sight.

As the fire fades, the past stands tall,
Echoes linger, they encompass all.
In ashes cold, a promise waits,
Time's breath whispers through the gates.

Finding peace in the remains,
The heart beats softly, yet still contains.
Life in layers, the cycle flows,
Time's breath lives where the silence grows.

Dreamscapes on the Edge of Dawn

In whispers soft, the shadows fade,
Colors bloom, as night is laid.
Chasing dreams on the horizon's line,
Awakening hearts, where hope does shine.

A gentle breeze stirs the waking trees,
With songs of light in the morning's tease.
Voices echo in the pastel sky,
As the world breathes in a new goodbye.

Through valleys deep, where silence lingers,
The dawn entwines with tender fingers.
Painted skies of peach and gold,
Unfolding stories, yet untold.

Lost in the hues, moments collide,
Where time stands still, and dreams abide.
A canvas stretched, with every hue,
The edge of dawn brings life anew.

So let us dance in the morning's grace,
Embracing wonders we shall face.
Each heartbeat marks this transient ride,
In dreamscapes wide, we shall abide.

Flickering Lights of the Silent Night

In the stillness, stars softly gleam,
Guiding lost souls, like a whispered dream.
Each twinkle tells of stories untold,
In the hush of night, mysteries unfold.

Moonlight drapes the world below,
Casting shadows, a gentle glow.
Fireflies dance through the quiet air,
Lighting paths without a care.

Whispers linger on the breath of trees,
Carrying secrets on the night's gentle breeze.
Every flicker, a fleeting embrace,
In the silence, we find our place.

The nightingale sings a lullaby sweet,
Where heartbeats and starlight meet.
Wrapped in darkness, dreams take flight,
Awake to the magic of the night.

As dawn approaches, shadows will play,
But the flickering lights will guide the way.
In the silence, we find a spark,
Illuminating paths in the dark.

Traces of Spirit in the Lingering Air

In the dusk, a sigh is heard,
Whispering tales without a word.
The essence lingers, soft and clear,
A gentle hug, always near.

Beneath the branches, secrets weave,
Echoes of spirits we believe.
Fragments dance on the twilight breeze,
Carried softly through ancient trees.

In shadows deep, where dreams might linger,
Time holds its breath with a tender finger.
Every moment, a sacred thread,
Woven through paths where angels tread.

In silent whispers, the past is drawn,
Painting the night, a delicate dawn.
Traces of spirit, love, and care,
In every heartbeat, everywhere.

So close your eyes and breathe it in,
Feel the warmth that lies within.
In the lingering air, we find our way,
Connected by love, come what may.

Symphonies of Starlight and Stillness

Beneath the curve of a velvet sky,
Whispers of starlight softly sigh.
In the quiet, a symphony plays,
Of nights unbroken, of timeless days.

Each star a note, in harmony bright,
Dancing to rhythms of tranquil night.
The moon, a conductor, guides the tune,
As dreams take flight beneath the moon.

In the hush of dusk, the heart finds peace,
A melody of stillness that will never cease.
Through twilight shadows, the echoes ring,
In the calm of evening, our spirits sing.

With every breath, we join the choir,
As hearts ignite with celestial fire.
Symphonies woven with love and grace,
In starlight's embrace, we find our place.

So let us dance in this gentle light,
Swaying together in the cool of night.
In the notes of silence, we shall be free,
In symphonies of starlight, you and me.

Echoes of a Cinder's Caress

In shadows deep where embers glow,
The whispers dance from long ago.
A fleeting touch, a subtle trace,
In every heart, a warm embrace.

The ashes stir, the night unfolds,
With secrets wrapped in silken folds.
A flicker bright in a world so vast,
Echoes linger, holding fast.

In silence we find what lies beneath,
The softness of a molten wreath.
Cinders fall like tears from stars,
Each drop reveals the pain of scars.

In shadows cast by fading fire,
We sing of loss, of lost desire.
Yet in the warmth, a spark remains,
A promise whispered through our pains.

Embers fade, but never die,
They dance in memory, soaring high.
In quiet hours, feel the glow,
Of cinder's caress, forever flow.

The Whispering Path of Fading Light

Along the lane where shadows creep,
The fading light begins to weep.
Soft whispers dance upon the air,
Inviting hearts to linger there.

The trees, they sway with secrets old,
Their stories waiting to be told.
Each step we take, the dusk unfolds,
Revealing dreams in twilight's gold.

A gentle breeze, a lover's sigh,
As fireflies light the evening sky.
The path ahead, uncertain still,
Yet beckons forth with tender thrill.

In silence found, reflections gleam,
Within the shadows, we dare to dream.
For in this hour of soft delight,
The whispering path feels just right.

Let go of doubts, embrace the glow,
As daylight fades, we learn to flow.
In every dusk, hope takes its flight,
On the whispering path of fading light.

Calm Reflections in a Broken Mirror

In shards of glass, a world divides,
With every crack, the truth hides.
Yet peace resides in fractured lines,
Where clarity and chaos intertwine.

Through splintered views, a glimpse of grace,
Reflections whisper in this space.
Each fragment tells a tale anew,
Of moments lost and struggles too.

What once was whole now tells a story,
Of broken dreams and faded glory.
Yet in the pieces, beauty lies,
A symphony of joyful cries.

A mirror fractured, yet so clear,
Inviting hearts to draw near.
In stillness found, we learn to see,
The calm within this mystery.

In quiet realms, we learn to find,
The beauty in a shattered mind.
For every break, a chance to start,
Calm reflections weave the heart.

Silent Flights of Imagined Wings

In dreams we soar on silent streams,
With whispered hopes and faded dreams.
Wings of thought take flight in air,
Carrying hearts beyond despair.

The clouds become our gentle steeds,
As freedom calls and thought proceeds.
Imagination paints the skies,
Where every spirit learns to rise.

Through realms unseen, we glide with grace,
In that great void, we find our place.
With every beat, our voices blend,
In symphonies that never end.

For in the silence lies the sound,
Of wings that lift from sacred ground.
Exploring heights we've yet to share,
In silent flights, we learn to care.

With every breeze, our spirits twine,
Imagined wings, forever shine.
In darkest nights, our dreams ignite,
On silent flights of pure delight.

Starlit Mystique of Restful Depths

In whispered night, the secrets dwell,
A canvas of dreams where shadows swell.
Crystals twinkling in velvet skies,
Inviting the heart, where silence lies.

Beneath the moon's soft, silver gaze,
The world transforms in evening's haze.
Ripples of calm flow through the air,
A sigh of stillness, a soothing prayer.

The depths of night in quiet sing,
Ode to the magic that darkness brings.
Stars weave tales in shimmering light,
Guiding the lost through endless night.

In dreams we wander, we drift, we soar,
Finding the peace we long for more.
Wrapped in the warmth of a slumbering sea,
The starlit mystique, forever free.

Embers Cradling Dreams on Soft Wings

Flickering flames in an evening glow,
Whispering tales from long ago.
Embers dance as the night unfolds,
Cradling dreams in their gentle holds.

On soft wings of whispers, we rise,
Carried away to the moonlit skies.
In the heart of night, our fears subside,
As the warmth of the embers becomes our guide.

With every spark, a story ignites,
Casting shadows that blur the nights.
Held by comfort, in silence we sway,
Dreams embedded in the close of day.

As stars take flight, the night will breathe,
Kissing the world with a soft reprieve.
In whispers we gather, boundless and free,
Embers cradling the dreams meant for thee.

A Gentle Dance Beneath the Lonely Stars

Beneath the stars, where shadows play,
A gentle dance leads the heart astray.
Soft melodies drift through the night,
Caressed by the glow of silver light.

In solitude's grace, we find our ground,
A rhythm of whispers, sweet and profound.
Each twirl a moment, fleeting yet pure,
The beauty of stillness, ours to endure.

Step by step, with grace we glide,
Hand in hand with the moon as our guide.
In the embrace of the starlit sighs,
We learn the language where silence flies.

Lost in the music of soft-spun dreams,
The universe holds us in sparkling beams.
With every heartbeat, a wish on the air,
A gentle dance, stripped of all care.

Time's Soft Embrace in the Twilight Sky

When twilight descends, the day grows old,
Time wraps us gently in twilight's fold.
Each moment lingers, sweet and deep,
Cradling us softly as we drift to sleep.

The horizon blurs in hues of gold,
Stories unfold that no one has told.
With each passing breath, we let go,
In time's soft embrace, the world moves slow.

Under the sky, so vast and grand,
We find ourselves in the burning sand.
Shadows stretch long, fading in grace,
While dreams take form in this sacred space.

In whispers of dusk, we start anew,
Time weaves its magic, tender and true.
Embracing the night with open hearts,
As twilight unveils its hidden arts.

Frosty Dawn on a Fiery Night

In the chill of the morn's breath,
Stars flicker their last light,
Awakening whispers of dreams,
Beneath a shroud of frost white.

Embers glow from the night's heart,
Orange skies blend with pale blue,
Nature stirs from a deep slumber,
As frost melts and day breaks through.

Shadows flicker in the cool air,
Echoes of warmth linger near,
Frosty dawn dances softly,
Past the remnants of night dear.

Hope rises with golden rays,
Each moment, a chance to ignite,
In the depth of the chill, we find,
A fiery warmth set alight.

Life awakes in a tender song,
As the dawn conquers the night,
In the frost's fleeting embrace,
A new beginning, pure and bright.

Tides of Stillness

Waves of calm surround the shore,
Whispers of peace in the breeze,
Moments linger, time drifts slow,
As hearts find solace with ease.

Footprints fade in the soft sand,
Memories wash with the tide,
Every breath a gentle touch,
Where secrets and dreams collide.

Sunset paints the sky in hues,
A canvas of serene retreat,
Colors blend in perfect harmony,
As day surrenders to night's greet.

In the stillness, echoes linger,
Moments caught in the ebb and flow,
Dancing shadows play with light,
Where time and eternity glow.

Tides retreat, yet they return,
From the vastness of life's sea,
In the stillness, hope remains,
Awakening that sets us free.

Waves of Memory

Ripples caress the quiet shore,
Memories swirl like ocean's tide,
Each wave brings a whispered name,
As time and distance collide.

Footprints linger in the sand,
Tales of laughter, joy, and pain,
The sea knows all our secrets,
Holding whispers of love's refrain.

Distant shores call to the weary,
Where the heart finds its long-lost home,
In waves of memory, we travel,
As tides of time gently roam.

Beneath the starlit skies above,
The moon reflects what once was whole,
Dancing waves, a soothing balm,
Healing every fractured soul.

In every ebb, we find our way,
Chasing dreams that softly blend,
Waves of memory wash over us,
In the heart, they never end.

Soft Light Between Ashen Shadows

In the dusk where shadows play,
Soft light flickers, gently glows,
Between the dark, a spark of hope,
Where silence whispers, yet it knows.

Ashen hues frame the twilight,
Each breath, a pause in the night,
Embers dance in the fading light,
Guiding souls from dark to bright.

Faint reflections on a still pond,
Where secrets swim beneath the sheen,
Soft light casts dreams upon the water,
In twilight's embrace, they convene.

Echoes of laughter, shadows lament,
Yet the soft light finds its way,
Illuminating the paths we walk,
In the heart's hidden ballet.

Between the ash and the glow,
Hope rises like the stars at night,
In every shadow lies a story,
Of soft light's everlasting fight.

Tranquil Twilight of the Hidden Flame

In twilight's hush, the world holds peace,
Where shadows stretch and time stands still,
A hidden flame flickers softly,
Stirring the heart with quiet thrill.

Soft hues blend in the fading light,
As day lends warmth to the night,
Each whisper of wind, a gentle song,
In the symphony of twilight's might.

Glimmers of gold dance on the leaves,
As nature sighs beneath the trees,
In twilight's grip, all worries cease,
Drawing solace from the evening breeze.

Hidden flames flicker in our souls,
Illuminating paths once lost,
With every heartbeat, every breath,
Awakens dreams, no matter the cost.

In tranquil moments, we find our way,
Through shadows that quietly fade,
A hidden flame, forever bright,
Guides us through every serenade.

Secrets of the Luminous Calm

In the stillness, whispers play,
A glow that softens the gray.
Stars flicker in a velvet night,
Holding secrets out of sight.

Gentle breezes weave their tune,
Crooning softly to the moon.
Dreams may linger, fade away,
But calm remains, night holds sway.

Shadows dance on tranquil streams,
Carrying the weight of dreams.
Each reflection tells a tale,
Of hopes that rise, of hearts that sail.

In this quiet, moments blend,
Where silence seems to befriend.
Unseen forces softly guide,
Through luminous calm, we abide.

A Dance of Dusky Petals

In twilight's grasp, they start to sway,
Dusky petals welcome the day.
A rustle soft, a fragrant bloom,
Waltzing away the hidden gloom.

With each heartbeat, colors twirl,
Nature's art begins to swirl.
A symphony of hues unfolds,
In dusky whispers, stories told.

Petals pirouette, wild and free,
Dancing under the old oak tree.
In every flutter, life ignites,
A celebration of warm nights.

As dusk enfolds the vibrant show,
In shadows deep, they gently flow.
A dance of whispers, soft and bright,
Carried forth by the coming night.

The Ghost of Forgotten Flames

In embers dim, a flicker waits,
Remnants of love behind the gates.
A ghostly warmth still haunts the air,
Echoes of passion, beyond compare.

Time has worn the fire down,
Yet shadows dance with a knowing frown.
Fragments linger, voices blend,
A symphony of hearts that mend.

Each sigh recalls a fleeting spark,
In the quiet, whispers mark.
Gone but not lost in the dark,
A silent echo, a lingering arc.

When twilight falls and memories rise,
Through the haze, the spirit flies.
In the breath of the night's embrace,
The ghost of flames finds its place.

Quiet Murmurs in the Heatwave

In the still heat, whispers hum,
Softly dancing, a secret drum.
Beneath the shimmer, stories wade,
In quiet murmur, dreams are made.

Golden sun wraps the world in heat,
With every step, the earth's heartbeat.
Leaves flutter in a gentle sigh,
As shadows linger, time slips by.

Moments melt into golden streams,
Where silence holds the weight of dreams.
In this hush, the world conspires,
To share with us its hidden fires.

The heatwave whispers, soft and low,
Carrying tales that ebb and flow.
In the warm embrace of the day,
Quiet murmurs lead the way.

Fantasies Woven in Ember's Threads

In the silence of the night, dreams take flight,
Whispers of the heart in shimmering light.
Threads of passion weave a tapestry bright,
Flickering shadows dance, a surreal sight.

Embers glow with secrets yet untold,
Carving paths of warmth through the cold.
In the tapestry, stories start to unfold,
Fantasies alive, a joy to behold.

Each spark a chapter, each flame a verse,
Breathing life into the universe.
In the depths of night, we softly rehearse,
Woven in ember, the soul's sweet immerse.

With every flicker, a memory keeps,
In the heart of the fire, the spirit leaps.
Embers of hopes, as the quiet now sleeps,
In a world of dreams, where wonder peeps.

Fantasies gleam in the fire's embrace,
Where time stands still, and we find our place.
Woven threads of light in this sacred space,
Ember's gentle glow, a lover's grace.

Resonance of the Fading Flames

As shadows grow long, the fire wanes,
Echoes of laughter in swirling lanes.
The heart remembers what the night contains,
In the fading light, the spirit gains.

Whispers of warmth in the cooling air,
Memories entwined like a lover's stare.
Resonance of time in a moment rare,
Fading flames rise, a luminescent flare.

The twilight wraps us in soft retreat,
Every heartbeat a whispered beat.
Fading flames draw us to our seat,
In the silence, our souls meet.

The night holds secrets in shadows deep,
In the glow of embers, our dreams we keep.
Resonance of love, as the heart does leap,
In the fading flames, where memories seep.

As darkness enfolds, the fire sighs,
Embers shiver under velvet skies.
In whispers of night, true beauty lies,
Fading flames tell the stories of our ties.

The Gentle Roar of Subtle Changes

In stillness found, the world begins to shift,
Gentle roars of change, a precious gift.
With every heartbeat, we find our drift,
Nature's song plays, as shadows lift.

Leaves fall softly, colors blaze and fade,
In the dance of time, a journey laid.
Whispers in the wind, decisions made,
Subtle changes, a serenade.

Moments like crystals, bright and clear,
Reflecting the paths that brought us here.
The gentle roar calls us to draw near,
Subtle changes whisper, unafraid to steer.

Seasons shift like the tides of fate,
In every heartbeat, we navigate.
The gentle roar hums, a calming state,
In subtle changes, love resonates.

With every dawn, a new story wakes,
A gentle reminder in every break.
The world in flux, beauty neverakes,
In the gentle roar, our spirit quakes.

Celestial Shadows in a Fire's Whisper

Under the stars, a fire flickers bright,
Celestial shadows paint the night.
In its warm glow, our souls take flight,
Whispers of the cosmos, a gentle light.

Every flame a story, in starlit dance,
Echoes of dreams in a cosmic trance.
Shadows entwined in a daring chance,
What we seek lies in this romance.

Fires crackle with secrets to unfold,
In every flicker, the universe bold.
Celestial whispers, treasures to behold,
In the night's embrace, our hearts consoled.

With each flicker, the night starts to sigh,
Celestial shadows roll softly by.
In the fire's whisper, we learn to fly,
Under the gaze of a thousand high.

As embers fade and the stars ignite,
We find our place in the depths of night.
Celestial shadows weave tales of light,
In a fire's whisper, dreams take flight.

The Breath of Life in Ashen Lullabies

In whispers soft, the night's caress,
Each breath a story, a gentle press.
From ashes rise, a warmth restored,
In lullabies where spirits soared.

The embers dance in fading light,
Echoes of dreams take flight in night.
Through velvet skies, the stars ignite,
Their shimmering paths, a guiding sight.

With every sigh, the heart's refrain,
Revives the lost, relieves the pain.
A cradle made of silent prayer,
Eternal love in evening air.

In ashen lullabies we trust,
To heal the weary, dream is must.
As shadows fold, we stand in grace,
Embrace the warmth, our sacred space.

So breathe the life in twilight's glow,
Amidst the softly falling snow.
In every turn, the cycle spins,
Within this peace, the heart begins.

Pensive Puffs of Evening Euphoria

Beneath the sky where colors blend,
The day in puffs begins to end.
A canvas rich, the dusk displayed,
Its euphoria, a drama played.

In twilight hush, the world exhales,
With every breath, the senses sail.
Through pensive thoughts of day's retreat,
The evening whispers, bittersweet.

Soft echoes linger in the air,
While shadows dance without a care.
As stars emerge with silver light,
They wrap the earth in velvet night.

In puffs of dreams, our hearts unite,
A symphony of sheer delight.
We grasp the moments, fleeting, rare,
In evening's glow, find solace there.

The world aglow, a magic sphere,
Where joy and wonder reappear.
In pensive puffs, we soar and sing,
A celebration of the spring.

Shadows at Rest in Ember's Glow

At night's embrace, where shadows dwell,
In ember's glow, they weave a spell.
A tranquil hush, the fire hums,
As weary hearts find peace that comes.

The world is draped in twilight's grace,
At rest, the stars take their place.
In silver beams, the moon ascends,
Wraps night in dreams as daylight ends.

Through flickering flames, stories rise,
In gentle whispers, love replies.
The past entwined, a tapestry,
As shadows dance in harmony.

In ember's glow, each soul takes flight,
Past burdens fade, trailing the night.
With every breath, new stories grow,
In shadows' arms, we learn to flow.

So close your eyes, and drift away,
In twilight's arms where we shall stay.
In peace, we find our hearts align,
In ember's glow, our dreams combine.

Blush of Twilight on the Phoenix's Wing

With every dusk, a blush unfolds,
On phoenix wings, a tale retold.
Through skies that shimmer, vibrant hue,
A dance of dreams and ashes too.

In twilight's grace, the day bids farewell,
A fleeting moment, a magic spell.
With colors rich, the horizon sighs,
As stars awaken in painted skies.

The phoenix soars, its flames aglow,
In quest of light, through night's soft flow.
Each feather bright, a story spun,
In twilight's arms, a new day's begun.

With wings outstretched, it greets the dawn,
In hope's embrace, the night is gone.
A blush ignites, the world reborn,
As shadows fade, a light is sworn.

So let us rise on wings of grace,
In twilight's blush, we find our place.
With every breath, we take to wing,
In life anew, hear the phoenix sing.

Laid-Back Whispers of the Ancient Flame

In the stillness, embers glow,
Ancient stories softly flow.
Whispers carried on the breeze,
Tales of warmth, of love, of ease.

Beneath the stars, the flame will dance,
Inviting hearts to take a chance.
In every flicker, a memory stays,
Echoing laughter, lost in days.

Quiet moments, time's embrace,
Flickering softly, a warm trace.
With every subtle crack and pop,
Life's gentle rhythm, it won't stop.

Embers fade but never die,
Smoking tendrils rising high.
Laid-back whispers, secrets shared,
In the glow, we find we cared.

So gather 'round, let voices blend,
In the flame, old wounds will mend.
With stories spun like threads of grace,
In the warmth, we find our place.

Serene Rays of Dusk and Dawn

The sun dips low, painting the sky,
With hues of orange, soft and spry.
Daylight wanes, a gentle sigh,
In dusk's embrace, all dreams can fly.

Morning breaks with tender light,
Kissing the world, dispelling night.
The dawn reveals a brand new start,
Awakening hope within the heart.

Nature whispers, a calming tune,
As shadows blend and flowers croon.
Each moment cherished, fleeting, rare,
Serene rays fill the silent air.

In twilight's glow, reflections gleam,
A tapestry unfolds, a dream.
With every sunrise, every set,
Beauty found, we won't forget.

So let the day and night entwine,
With gentle grace, a sacred line.
In every hue, in every breath,
Serene rays conquer life and death.

Celestial Hush Over the Smoldering Earth

The world lies still, a breathless pause,
Under cosmic lights, life's cause.
Stars awake to watch and twirl,
As the earth smolders, dreams unfurl.

In night's embrace, secrets lay,
Whispers carried far away.
A celestial hush blankets the ground,
In this silence, peace is found.

Fire crackles like distant thoughts,
In the stillness, time entwines knots.
Smoldering embers, flickering bright,
A dance of shadow, a play of light.

Galaxies spin in the cosmic sea,
While nature sleeps, wild and free.
The quiet echoes speak of birth,
Celestial hush over the smoldering earth.

Beneath the stars, we find our place,
In this vast, infinite embrace.
With every breath, we feel the weight,
Of life, of love, and our shared fate.

Silent Footsteps on the Path of Flames

Through the embers, shadows creep,
Silent footsteps, secrets keep.
The ground ignites with tales untold,
Of brave hearts and spirits bold.

Every crackle calls us near,
In the night, we feel no fear.
Walking softly, feeling the heat,
In the rhythm where fire and earth meet.

The path winds on, a fiery glow,
Illuminates the dreams we sow.
In every step, a story we weave,
Of hopes ignited, dreams believed.

Dance of shadows, embrace the flame,
In the silence, whisper a name.
A journey forged on molten ground,
In every heartbeat, love is found.

So tread with care, embrace the night,
For the path of flames shines ever bright.
With every step, courage reclaim,
In silent footsteps, we rise, untamed.

Whispers of the Embered Dawn

In the quiet of the morn,
Soft lights begin to play,
Whispers dance through leaves,
A brand new day in sway.

Sunrise paints the horizon,
With hues of gold and red,
Nature breathes a secret,
As dreams recede from bed.

Clouds drift like gentle echoes,
Carried on the breeze,
The world awakens slowly,
Finding calm in ease.

Birds sing to greet the dawning,
Their melodies take flight,
Each note a soft reminder,
Of beauty within light.

The fireflies bid farewell,
To shadows of the night,
With every glimmer fading,
A promise to ignite.

The Stillness Between Wings

In the hush of twilight hour,
Silence wraps the sky,
Dreams drift down like feathers,
Whispers softly fly.

Wings of dusk unfurl gently,
Creating space to breathe,
Between the old and new,
Where magic finds belief.

Stars awaken from their slumber,
Twinkling with delight,
In shadows softly weaving,
Nighttime's soft invite.

With every breath, a moment,
A chance to feel it all,
The stillness wraps around me,
In night's tender call.

Time bows to the silence,
As hearts begin to soar,
Within the calm between us,
We find a world to explore.

Echoes of Serene Winds

Whispers flow through ancient trees,
With stories to unfold,
The winds carry their secrets,
In breaths both soft and bold.

Each rustle tells of wanderers,
Who passed beneath the boughs,
The echoes linger softly,
In nature's gentle vows.

Mountains hum a timeless tune,
As rivers weave their spell,
In harmony with silence,
Where peace and beauty dwell.

The sky embraces twilight,
With hues of purple grace,
Where every breeze feels timeless,
In stillness, we find space.

As shadows join the chorus,
A lullaby takes flight,
In echoes of the winds,
We dance until the night.

Hushed Currents in the Twilight

As dusk descends upon the land,
The world begins to slow,
Hushed currents gently flow,
Where dreams and shadows grow.

The river sings a soft refrain,
Its waters calm and deep,
While memories like drifting leaves,
In twilight's arms, we keep.

Stars glimmer in the quiet sky,
A tapestry of night,
Each twinkle holds a secret,
Beneath the silver light.

Between the whispers of the trees,
A painter's brush will kiss,
The canvas of the evening,
Where silence tastes like bliss.

In the hush of twilight magic,
We find a place to dwell,
In the currents ever fleeting,
Where the heart knows all is well.

Solitude Among the Radiant Breach

In a silent wood, I tread alone,
Whispers of nature, a gentle tone.
Light filters through, like dreams of gold,
Stories of silence, waiting to be told.

The air is thick, with unspoken vows,
As shadows dance, and the daylight bows.
Each step I take, a memory wakes,
In this radiant breach, my spirit takes.

Among the trees, where the wild things play,
Time drifts softly, like clouds in gray.
Lost in reverie, I find my peace,
In solitude's arms, my worries cease.

The rustling leaves, my only friends,
In this tranquil hush, where time bends.
I breathe in deep, and feel the space,
Solitude's grace leaves a simple trace.

As evening falls, colors start to blend,
The sun whispers soft, the day's sweet end.
In this radiant breach, I find my home,
Among the quiet, forever I'll roam.

The Emptiness After the Fire

Once bright flames danced, now ashes lie,
A charred remains beneath the sky.
Whispers of heat linger in the air,
Echoes of passion, sparks of despair.

Gone are the nights filled with fervent light,
Only shadows haunt, a ghostly sight.
The warmth is replaced by a chilling breeze,
An emptiness blooms, with disquieting ease.

Memories flicker, like embers that fade,
In the silence, I start to feel played.
What once was whole, now fragmented space,
The heart aches to find a familiar face.

But in the void, a strange beauty grows,
Out of the dark, a resilience flows.
From ashes we rise, from silence we sing,
The emptiness bears what rebirth can bring.

So I gather my strength, piece by piece,
In the aftermath, I seek my release.
For each end bears a promise anew,
In the emptiness, I find my view.

Sighs of the Eternal Phoenix

From the depths of night, a whisper begins,
The phoenix awakens, shedding its sins.
With a roar of fire that breaks the air,
It soars through the heavens, igniting despair.

Wings spread wide, like the dawn's embrace,
Leaving behind frustrations, finding grace.
In the ashes of yesterday's fight,
It seeks out the stars, igniting the night.

Each sigh it breathes, carries dreams untold,
In a cycle of passion, fierce and bold.
Born of the flames, reborn in the light,
Eternal as time, it conquers the night.

With every rebirth, the heart learns to heal,
In the echoes of struggle, strength is revealed.
So let the fires burn, let them consume,
For from the ashes, the phoenix finds bloom.

In the sighs of the combat, life takes its stand,
Guided by forces, unseen by the hand.
With unwavering spirit, it rises once more,
The eternal phoenix, forever to soar.

Serenities of the Westward Gale

The westward gale comes, with whispers so light,
Caressing the fields, it's a beautiful sight.
Carried on breezes of lavender hues,
It dances through meadows, brushing the dews.

Through valleys it flows, with a gentle embrace,
Calling the wildflowers, leading their grace.
A symphony plays, as each petal sways,
In the serenities of long, golden days.

Resting my soul in the soft, summer air,
Nature surrounds me; I have worries to spare.
Each sigh of the gale serves to remind,
Of peace in the chaos, how love is designed.

As twilight unfolds, a canvas of stars,
The wind carries dreams, like forgotten memoirs.
In the calm of the night, the world holds its breath,
In serenities found, is the essence of rest.

So let the gale sing, let its spirit be free,
For in every whisper, there's solace for me.
In the westward's embrace, I find my place,
Where the world and the heart entwine with grace.

Lullabies Beneath the Sulfur Sun

In shadows dance the fireflies bright,
With whispers soft as fading light.
They sing the tales of dusk's embrace,
While stars emerge in velvet space.

The sulfur sun dips low in skies,
A canvas painted with goodbyes.
The world wraps in a tender shroud,
Where silence stands as dreams are loud.

Beneath the warmth of warming glow,
The night unfolds, its secrets flow.
Each lullaby a calming balm,
In darkness finds the heart a calm.

So let the evening's hush descend,
With gentle sighs that seem to blend.
In twilight's arms, we softly sway,
As night consumes the dying day.

And in this space, we find our rest,
With lullabies that feel the best.
Beneath the sulfur sun we lay,
In slumber's grasp until the day.

Sheltered Whispers of the Cinder Hill

Upon the hill of ashes gray,
Sheltered whispers come to play.
The softest breezes brush the air,
With secrets spoken everywhere.

Each ember glows with stories told,
Of fiery nights and hearts so bold.
The cinder hill holds hopes anew,
With every sigh, a life we drew.

And in this warmth, we find our peace,
As shadows dance and worries cease.
The world outside may churn and fight,
Here, in this stillness, all feels right.

Cinder dreams in twilight fade,
As whispers form in masquerade.
A language known to hearts that hear,
In whispered love, there's naught to fear.

So gather close, let firelight glow,
In sheltered realms, our spirits flow.
The cinder hill will keep us warm,
Through every storm, our hearts transform.

Embraced by the Sigh of Sundown

In amber hues the day retreats,
As twilight unfolds its soft defeats.
The sigh of sundown calls us near,
With whispered dreams that calm our fear.

The horizon blushes, shyly speaks,
In colors bold, the silence leaks.
Between the moments time stands still,
In evening's arms, we find our thrill.

Embraced by whispers sweet and low,
The sun dips low, a gentle flow.
With every breath, the world unwinds,
As night conceals what daylight finds.

Beneath this canopy of grace,
Our shadows shift, a warm embrace.
In every dusk, new dreams ignite,
As hearts entwine in soft twilight.

So close your eyes and feel the pull,
As sundown sighs, our hearts are full.
Embraced by night, we drift away,
In dreams that rise with night's ballet.

Tender Murmurs of the Charred Meadow

In charred meadows where silence reigns,
Tender murmurs hide the pains.
The earth remembers, scarring deep,
While nature sings a song of sleep.

Amongst the ashes, life still thrives,
In whispered tones, the spirit strives.
Each leaf a testament of time,
In every breath, a gentle rhyme.

The twilight softens every scar,
As constellations light the far.
With open hearts, we learn to heal,
And find the truth in what we feel.

So gather close upon the land,
With tender murmurs, hand in hand.
We build anew from what was lost,
In charred meadows, we pay the cost.

Together, we find solace here,
In whispered thoughts that calm our fear.
In every breath, a promise made,
In charred meadows, dreams won't fade.

Moments Caught in Transient Air

Whispers dance upon the breeze,
Fragments of laughter weave through trees.
Time hangs lightly, a feathered sigh,
Captured dreams as the moments fly.

Sunlight flickers in the open field,
A tapestry of light revealed.
Chasing shadows where secrets play,
In the transient air, we drift away.

Echoes of voices, softly call,
In the stillness, we stand tall.
Each heartbeat marks a brief embrace,
Memories linger in this space.

Fleeting glances, a touch of grace,
In these moments, we find our place.
Time, a river, flowing fast,
But in each breath, a spell is cast.

As dusk descends, the stars appear,
Filling our hearts with quiet cheer.
In the transient air, we are free,
Floating softly, eternally.

Nature's Breath Amidst Forgotten Ruins

Amidst the stones of ages past,
Nature breathes, her beauty vast.
Leaves entwined with crumbled walls,
In silent grace, her spirit calls.

Vines embrace what time obscured,
In whispered tones, the heart is lured.
Petals fall where shadows creep,
In ruins, ancient secrets sleep.

A lonely bird sings soft and low,
Filling the air with tales of woe.
Crumbling arches, a silent choir,
Beneath the sky, we rise, inspire.

Echoes of laughter on the stone,
In nature's breath, we feel at home.
Moonlight dances on faded tomes,
Among the ruins, our spirit roams.

Life finds a way to softly bloom,
Despite the shadows of impending gloom.
Nature heals what once was torn,
In forgotten ruins, we are reborn.

The Soft Revolution of Burning Time

Embers flicker in the quiet night,
Time unfolds in gentle light.
Each moment seems to softly glow,
In the revolution, we ebb and flow.

Seconds stretch into fleeting dreams,
As the world, a tapestry seams.
With every tick, a story spun,
Life ignites, and we become one.

The spark of hope, a tender flame,
Inside our hearts, we feel the same.
Dancing shadows in the twilight,
In burning time, we find our flight.

Seasons turn in soft refrain,
Whispers echo through joy and pain.
The clock unravels, yet we choose,
In burning time, we cannot lose.

A symphony of moments collide,
As dreams and memories coincide.
In the soft revolution, we ignite,
Together, we embrace the night.

Idyllic Silence Between the Flames

In a world where chaos reigns,
We seek the peace that still remains.
Between the flames, a quiet breath,
Idyllic silence, resisting death.

Crackling warmth, a gentle sound,
Stories linger, lost and found.
In the glow, a tranquil heart,
Between each flicker, love imparts.

Amidst the fire's fierce embrace,
We find solace, our resting place.
Wrapped in warmth, a tender thread,
In silence, the words left unsaid.

Each flame a beacon in the night,
Guiding us toward the soft light.
In this space, we breathe in dreams,
Finding peace in life's extremes.

As embers fade, the stars will shine,
In idyllic silence, our hearts align.
Together through the tempest's dance,
Between the flames, we find romance.

Serene Flows of Celestial Currents

In the stillness of the night,
Stars whisper soft delights,
Moonlight weaves through trees,
Dancing shadows on the leaves.

Water glistens in the dark,
Rippling gently, leaving marks,
Echoes of the calmest peace,
Cradled in the night's release.

Clouds drift lazily above,
Carrying dreams and love,
Each breath a soothing wave,
Guiding hearts they gently save.

Night blooms with a quiet grace,
Time slows in this sacred space,
Whispers of the cosmic flow,
Calmness in the starlight glow.

In this realm where heartbeats blend,
Nature's lullabies suspend,
Floating on celestial streams,
Finding peace in tranquil dreams.

Tranquil Currents Under Starlit Dreams

Beneath the stars' embracing light,
Whispers cradle the serene night,
Waves of peace, a soft embrace,
Sleepy shadows find their place.

Gentle streams meander down,
Kissing earth with nature's crown,
Reflections of a world unseen,
In silver sparkles, dreams convene.

Moonbeams waltz on tranquil tides,
Where secrets of the stillness hide,
Every rustle, every sigh,
A symphony as breezes fly.

Lost in wonders, all is clear,
Embracing night, there's naught to fear,
Stars align in silent schemes,
Igniting the heart with dreams.

In this hush, let spirits soar,
To realms unknown, forevermore,
With each breath, the night unfolds,
Boundless tales that time beholds.

Secrets Carried by the Gentle Air

Softly speaks the evening breeze,
Carrying tales of ancient trees,
Between the leaves, whispers blend,
Nature's song, a timeless friend.

Across the hills, the shadows creep,
In twilight's glow, we softly leap,
Echoes dance on fragrant blooms,
In the air, the magic looms.

Feathers drift on currents free,
Telling stories to land and sea,
The rustle holds a sacred trust,
In every gust, a secret gust.

Listen close; the night is wise,
In every sigh, new worlds arise,
Gentle air, a lullaby,
Whispered truths beneath the sky.

Each breath taken, sacred gift,
As the stars begin to lift,
Through the night, the echoes flow,
In the softest winds, we grow.

Soft Songs from the Ashen Heights

From the heights where silence sings,
Echoes cradle gentle wings,
Softly woven, tales unfold,
In shadows where the night is bold.

The ash trees sway with whispered grace,
Holding secrets of this place,
In rustling leaves, soft prayers rise,
A harmony that fills the skies.

Moonlit paths through ashen trails,
Where the nightingale prevails,
Each note a kiss upon the air,
Soft reminders, frail and rare.

Breezes carry stories lost,
In the twilight's gentle frost,
Phantoms dance in midnight's hue,
In soft songs, our souls renew.

Up high where dreams take flight,
Every heart finds pure delight,
Under stars, we drift and sway,
Listening to what night will say.

The Stillness Between the Heartbeats

In silence deep, a pause remains,
Where whispers fade, yet love still gains.
A gentle sigh, a fleeting thought,
The sacred space that time forgot.

In twilight's glow, emotions blend,
With every beat, beginnings mend.
The heart's soft pulse, a tender song,
In stillness, we know we belong.

A moment captured, breath held tight,
The world slow dances, day to night.
In this embrace, the shadows play,
Holding close what words can't say.

Lost in gazes that intertwine,
The vast unknown, a sacred line.
Through silence thick, the truth does rise,
In close proximity, love defies.

So linger here, where hearts reside,
In the stillness, forever side by side.
For in each heartbeat, a truth unfolds,
A bond that whispers, never grows cold.

Golden Gleams of Twilight's Breath

The sky ignites in fiery hues,
As day concedes with soft goodbyes.
Golden beams dance on the dew,
As dusk unveils its velvet sighs.

A quiet magic fills the air,
With every shade, a tale retells.
Whispers linger in the fair,
Where twilight gathers, silence dwells.

Crickets sing their evening hymn,
While fireflies twinkle, nature's stars.
In this moment, dusk feels brimmed,
With secrets held in fading bars.

The horizon glows with warmth anew,
A canvas brushed with love and grace.
Each golden gleam, a promise true,
In twilight's arms, we find our place.

So here we stand, the world at rest,
Where time is swallowed by the night.
In golden gleams, we are blessed,
As dreams take flight in fading light.

Shadows Dancing on Embered Ground

Beneath the stars, the shadows sway,
On embered ground where whispers roam.
A flicker here, a dance to play,
In twilight's grasp, we find our home.

The flames lick high, their secrets cast,
In flickering light, the past returns.
They tell of times both deep and vast,
Of love unnoticed, yet brightly burns.

A haunting tune that stirs the night,
In every crackle, souls entwine.
The shadows move with whispered light,
In every heart, a flicker shines.

So gather close, let stories weave,
Around the flames that softly glow.
In shadows dancing, we believe,
That love endures, and hope still grows.

Together here, the embers gleam,
In plush embrace, we blend our sound.
For every shadow holds a dream,
On embered ground, our hearts are found.

Lullabies Beneath the Smoldering Horizon

The sun dips low, a fiery crest,
As night unfolds with gentle grace.
Lullabies weave in golden rest,
Beneath the stars, a soft embrace.

The horizon glows with dying light,
As shadows whisper in the dusk.
In every breeze, a sweet invite,
To lose ourselves in twilight's husk.

Stars awaken, one by one,
As crickets join the evening's song.
Beneath the weight of day now done,
We cradle dreams where we belong.

The world grows still, a tender pause,
In twilight's hue, our spirits soar.
With every note, we start to cause,
The heart to listen, yearn for more.

So let the night embrace our fears,
With lullabies that softly play.
In slumber, weave our hopes and tears,
Beneath the smoldering sky, we stay.

Echoed Dreams of the Celestial Dawn

In the hush of morning light,
Whispers of dreams take flight.
Stars fade in soft embrace,
As the sun claims its place.

Colors bloom in the sky,
As night graciously says goodbye.
Echoes of laughter swirl,
In a world that starts to twirl.

Each breath a brand new start,
Awakening the sleeping heart.
Hope dances on the breeze,
Carried by the waking trees.

With open arms, we greet,
The rhythm of life's heartbeat.
As shadows melt away,
We welcome the break of day.

In the brilliance, dreams take form,
A promise in the quiet storm.
A symphony of light and grace,
Echoes linger, find their place.

A Gentle Fondness for the Night's Embrace

Underneath a velvet sky,
Stars twinkle like a sigh.
Moonlight drapes the world in peace,
As worries slowly cease.

Whispers born on midnight air,
Calling hearts to show they care.
With shadows casting tales that glow,
In the night's soft, tender flow.

A gentle fondness found in dreams,
Where nothing's quite as it seems.
Between the silence, moments weave,
A magic that we all believe.

The cool breeze breathes a soft caress,
In the dark, we find our rest.
Every sigh, a lullaby,
As stars share their secrets high.

In night's embrace, we lose our way,
But always find the light of day.
Wrapped in shadows, still we bloom,
Our hearts alight through every room.

The Stillness of Shadows in Luminous Circles

In corners where secrets dwell,
Whispers weave a silent spell.
Shadows dance in quiet grace,
In luminous circles, find their place.

Beneath the gaze of silver light,
They swirl in patterns, taking flight.
Mysteries wrapped in soft embrace,
A grand performance, time's own pace.

Stillness holds a breath so deep,
As night unveils what dreams can keep.
A canvas drawn with light's own hand,
A world inspired, vast and grand.

In shadows thick, wisdom lies,
Beneath the watchful, brilliant skies.
Each flicker, a story to share,
Painting visions in the air.

Every moment, a chance to see,
The beauty in shadows, wild and free.
In luminous circles, we find our way,
As night transforms and greets the day.

Lost Whispers of a Fiery Phoenix

From ashes deep, a flicker born,
A legend rises, reborn.
With wings of flame, it takes to flight,
In the darkest depth of night.

Lost whispers call from the past,
In a dance that's moving fast.
Each ember glows with tales untold,
A fire's heart, both fierce and bold.

Fires extinguished, yet they gleam,
Carrying the weight of a dream.
In every rise, a story speaks,
Of trials faced and courage peaks.

Through the smoke, the truth breaks free,
A phoenix sings in harmony.
Its song a balm for weary souls,
Igniting hope and making whole.

In lost whispers of the night,
We find our strength to fight the fight.
A fiery spirit wrapped in grace,
In every heart, it finds its place.

Veils of Mist Over Forgotten Plains

Veils of mist descend so light,
Whispers dance in morning's might.
Secrets held in nature's sigh,
Forgotten tales as shadows fly.

The grasses bow beneath their weight,
Weaving dreams of love and fate.
Echoes linger in the air,
Timeless stories, soft and rare.

Beneath the sun, the figures fade,
Past and present softly wade.
Silhouettes of those long gone,
Fade like twilight, dusk's sweet song.

In every fold, a memory waits,
Silent songs that time narrates.
Each breath taken on this ground,
In the mist, lost souls are found.

Through the haze, a spirit runs,
Chasing dreams beneath the suns.
Very little remains of old,
But the stories still are told.

Delicate Breath of Memory's Touch

In the silence, whispers gleam,
Fragrant echoes of a dream.
Each memory, a tender thread,
Woven soft in hearts we tread.

The past enfolds like gentle air,
Time's embrace, a lover's care.
Fleeting moments hold their sway,
Guiding footsteps on their way.

Shadows linger close and near,
Brushing softly, drawing near.
In every heartbeat, stories wake,
Life's mosaic, memories make.

Faintest sighs, a breeze's call,
Reminders of the rise and fall.
A tapestry of laughter spun,
Memories, two, become as one.

In veins of time, these feelings flow,
A secret dance, a soft tableau.
The delicate breath of days gone by,
Whispers of love that never die.

Unseen Threads of the Phoenix's Heart

From ashes rise a fiery glow,
Unseen threads where spirits flow.
Strength of heart, rebirth begins,
Hope's warm light, the journey spins.

In shadows cast by endless night,
Flickers of the spirit's light.
A flame ignites with fervent grace,
Transcending time, a sacred space.

With every beat, the heart will soar,
Through the heavens, seek to explore.
Stars align, their paths entwined,
A story woven, fate designed.

Rising high above the pain,
The Phoenix sings through sun and rain.
From every tear, a dream is born,
In flight, the spirit's grace is worn.

Embers dance beneath the sky,
A testament that we can fly.
Life renews in vibrant art,
Unseen threads of the Phoenix's heart.

Murmurs in the Twilight's Embrace

In twilight's soft and gentle hold,
Murmurs weave through stories told.
Fleeting moments linger low,
As day prepares to let night flow.

A canvas brushed with hues of grey,
The sun dips low, then fades away.
Stars awaken, one by one,
In echoing strains of day's last run.

Whispers float on evening's breeze,
Time stands still, our hearts at ease.
Reflections dance in muted light,
Dreams unfurl in the quiet night.

The shadows stretch, the world asleep,
Secrets kept, our hearts do keep.
In every sigh, a bond we trace,
Murmurs linger in twilight's embrace.

A chorus sung by night's sweet hymn,
Connects the edges, soft and dim.
With hope anew, the dreamers stand,
In twilight's grace, we join hands.

Subdued Chants of Rising Ash

The embers whisper soft and low,
Carried by winds that roam and flow.
In twilight's grasp, the shadows sway,
As fading light begins to play.

A cloak of gray wraps around the night,
While stars emerge, a distant light.
In quiet breaths, the ashes rise,
Our hopes entwined with whispered sighs.

A symphony of loss and gain,
Each flicker tales of joy and pain.
They dance amidst the twilight's blush,
In this stillness, time turns to hush.

The world finds peace in falling dust,
In quiet trust, we learn to adjust.
As whispers cease and silence grows,
The heart remembers what it knows.

In shadows deep, new dreams are spun,
With every breath, a journey begun.
So let the ash cover the ground,
In quietude, our souls are found.

Muffled Echoes Beneath a Crimson Sky

Beneath the hues of crimson splendor,
Where twilight's breath feels warm and tender.
In hushed tones the shadows creep,
Where secrets linger, silence deep.

The echoes dance on the evening breeze,
Among the rustling, whispering trees.
They hold the stories of days gone by,
In every sigh, in every cry.

A tapestry woven of dusk and dreams,
Life spills gently, like silver streams.
As colors fade, the night unfolds,
In muffled rhythms, the heart holds.

The sky ignites with a fleeting flame,
Each moment cherished, never the same.
In twilight's arms, we find our way,
Through whispers lost in yesterday.

In the depths of night, beneath the stars,
We gather the echoes, our silent memoirs.
Muffled songs in the cool night air,
United in dreams we silently share.

Tranquil Moments in a Pyre's Glow

A gentle fire flickers bright,
In the stillness of the night.
Its warmth embraces, calm and slow,
In tranquil moments, hearts will grow.

The flames dance softly, stories told,
In glowing whispers, brave and bold.
Each spark a memory, rich and clear,
In the pyre's glow, we draw near.

Surrounded by shadows, time suspends,
As hope ignites and life transcends.
In flickering light, we chase away
The fears that linger from yesterday.

The embers fade, yet still they spark,
Illumination breaks the dark.
In silent reverie, spirits soar,
With grateful hearts, we seek for more.

In every moment, a chance to see,
The bonds of love that set us free.
In the pyre's glow, we stand in awe,
Embracing life, our souls in raw.

Still Reflections in the Blazing Haze

In blazing haze, the world feels dreamt,
Through shimmering light, our senses wept.
Reflections dance upon the lake,
In stillness found, we gently wake.

The sun hangs low, a golden sphere,
As shadows stretch, they fade from here.
Each ripple carries a distant thought,
In silent moments, peace is caught.

The air is thick with warmth and light,
As echoes of day give way to night.
Still reflections upon mirrored glass,
Whispering tales of moments past.

In quietude where dreams align,
Time stands still, a gentle sign.
Embrace the now, let worries part,
In blazing haze, we find our heart.

The world may swirl in chaos loud,
But in this moment, we stand proud.
With stillness held, the heart can sing,
In blazing haze, new life takes wing.

www.ingramcontent.com/pod-product-compliance
Lightning Source LLC
Chambersburg PA
CBHW071536290125
21070CB00032B/810